BLANK NEWSPAPER ARTICLES

SPECIAL REPORT EDITION!

SPECIAL REPORT

EXTRA! EXTRA!

DATE: _____________

ABOUT THE AUTHOR

READ ALL ABOUT IT!

SPECIAL REPORT

50

EXTRA!
EXTRA!

(NAME OF PAPER)

DATE: _______________

(HEADLINE)

(WEATHER HEADLINE)

(DRAWING OF EVENT)

(EVENT DETAILS)

ABOUT THE AUTHOR

(ABOUT ME)

READ ALL ABOUT IT!

SPECIAL REPORT

EXTRA!
EXTRA!

DATE: _______________

ABOUT THE AUTHOR

READ ALL ABOUT IT!

SPECIAL REPORT

50

EXTRA! EXTRA!

(NAME OF PAPER)

DATE: _____________

(HEADLINE) _____________

(WEATHER HEADLINE) _____________

(DRAWING OF EVENT)

(EVENT DETAILS)

ABOUT THE AUTHOR

(ABOUT ME)

READ ALL ABOUT IT!

SPECIAL REPORT

50

EXTRA!
EXTRA!

DATE: _______________

ABOUT THE AUTHOR

READ ALL ABOUT IT!

SPECIAL REPORT

(NAME OF PAPER)

DATE: _______________

(HEADLINE)

(WEATHER HEADLINE)

(DRAWING OF EVENT)

(EVENT DETAILS)

ABOUT THE AUTHOR

(ABOUT ME)

READ ALL ABOUT IT!

SPECIAL REPORT

50

EXTRA! EXTRA!

DATE: ________________

ABOUT THE AUTHOR

READ ALL ABOUT IT!

SPECIAL REPORT

EXTRA! EXTRA!

50

(NAME OF PAPER)

DATE: ______________

(HEADLINE)

(WEATHER HEADLINE)

(DRAWING OF EVENT)

(EVENT DETAILS)

ABOUT THE AUTHOR

(ABOUT ME)

READ ALL ABOUT IT!

SPECIAL REPORT

50

EXTRA! EXTRA!

DATE: ___________

ABOUT THE AUTHOR

READ ALL ABOUT IT!

SPECIAL REPORT

50

EXTRA! EXTRA!

(NAME OF PAPER)

DATE: _______________

(HEADLINE)
____

(WEATHER HEADLINE)
____

(DRAWING OF EVENT)

(EVENT DETAILS)

ABOUT THE AUTHOR

(ABOUT ME)

READ ALL ABOUT IT!

SPECIAL REPORT

EXTRA! EXTRA!

50

DATE: _______________

ABOUT THE AUTHOR

READ ALL ABOUT IT!

SPECIAL REPORT

50

EXTRA! EXTRA!

(NAME OF PAPER)

DATE: _______________

(HEADLINE)

(WEATHER REPORT)

(DRAWING OF EVENT)

(EVENT DETAILS)

ABOUT THE AUTHOR

(ABOUT ME)

READ ALL ABOUT IT!

SPECIAL REPORT

50

EXTRA! EXTRA!

DATE: _______________

ABOUT THE AUTHOR

READ ALL ABOUT IT!

SPECIAL REPORT

50

EXTRA! EXTRA!

(NAME OF PAPER)

DATE: ___________

(HEADLINE)

(WEATHER HEADLINE)

(DRAWING OF EVENT)

(EVENT DETAILS)

ABOUT THE AUTHOR

(ABOUT ME)

READ ALL ABOUT IT!

SPECIAL REPORT

50

EXTRA! EXTRA!

DATE: _______________

ABOUT THE AUTHOR

READ ALL ABOUT IT!

SPECIAL REPORT

50

EXTRA! EXTRA!

(NAME OF PAPER)

DATE: ______________

(HEADLINE)

(WEATHER HEADLINE)

(DRAWING OR EVENT)

(EVENT DETAILS)

ABOUT THE AUTHOR

(ABOUT ME)

READ ALL ABOUT IT!

SPECIAL REPORT

50

EXTRA! EXTRA!

DATE: ___________

ABOUT THE AUTHOR

READ ALL ABOUT IT!

SPECIAL REPORT

EXTRA! EXTRA!

(NAME OF PAPER)

DATE: ______________

(HEADLINE)

(WEATHER HEADLINE)

(DRAWING OF EVENT)

(EVENT DETAILS)

ABOUT THE AUTHOR

(ABOUT ME)

READ ALL ABOUT IT!

SPECIAL REPORT

50

EXTRA! EXTRA!

DATE: _______________

ABOUT THE AUTHOR

READ ALL ABOUT IT!

SPECIAL REPORT

50

EXTRA! EXTRA!

(NAME OF PAPER)

DATE: ______________

(HEADLINE) ________________

(WEATHER HEADLINE) ________________

(DRAWING OF EVENT)

(EVENT DETAILS)

____

ABOUT THE AUTHOR

(ALL ABOUT ME)

READ ALL ABOUT IT!

50

SPECIAL REPORT

EXTRA! EXTRA!

DATE: _______________

ABOUT THE AUTHOR

READ ALL ABOUT IT!

SPECIAL REPORT

EXTRA!
EXTRA!

50

(NAME OF PAPER)

DATE: _______________

(HEADLINE)

(WEATHER HEADLINE)

(DRAWING OF EVENT)

(EVENT DETAILS)

ABOUT THE AUTHOR

(ABOUT ME)

READ ALL ABOUT IT!

SPECIAL REPORT

50

EXTRA! EXTRA!

DATE: ___________

ABOUT THE AUTHOR

READ ALL ABOUT IT!

SPECIAL REPORT

EXTRA! EXTRA!

50

(NAME OF PAPER)

DATE: __________

(HEADLINE) __________

(WEATHER HEADLINE) __________

(DRAWING OF EVENT)

(EVENT DETAILS)

ABOUT THE AUTHOR

(ABOUT ME)

READ ALL ABOUT IT!

SPECIAL REPORT

50

EXTRA! EXTRA!

DATE: _____________

ABOUT THE AUTHOR

READ ALL ABOUT IT!

SPECIAL REPORT

50

EXTRA! EXTRA!

(NAME OF PAPER)

DATE: _______________

(HEADLINE)

(WEATHER HEADLINE)

(DRAWING OF EVENT)

(EVENT DETAILS)

ABOUT THE AUTHOR

(ABOUT ME)

READ ALL ABOUT IT!

SPECIAL REPORT

DATE: ___________

ABOUT THE AUTHOR

READ ALL ABOUT IT!

SPECIAL REPORT

50

EXTRA! EXTRA!

(NAME OF PAPER)

DATE: _______________

(HEADLINE) _______________

(WEATHER FORECAST) _______________

(DRAWING OF EVENT)

(EVENT DETAILS)

ABOUT THE AUTHOR

(ABOUT ME)

READ ALL ABOUT IT!

SPECIAL REPORT

50

EXTRA!
EXTRA!

DATE: _______________

ABOUT THE AUTHOR

READ ALL ABOUT IT!

SPECIAL REPORT

50

EXTRA! EXTRA!

(NAME OF PAPER)

DATE: ______________

(HEADLINE)

(WEATHER HEADLINE)

(DRAWING OF EVENT)

(EVENT DETAILS)

ABOUT THE AUTHOR

(ABOUT ME)

READ ALL ABOUT IT!

SPECIAL REPORT

50

EXTRA!
EXTRA!

DATE: ______________

ABOUT THE AUTHOR

READ ALL ABOUT IT!

SPECIAL REPORT

(NAME OF PAPER)

DATE: ______________

(HEADLINE)

(WEATHER HEADLINE)

(DRAWING OF EVENT)

(EVENT DETAILS)

ABOUT THE AUTHOR

(ABOUT ME)

READ ALL ABOUT IT!

SPECIAL REPORT

EXTRA! EXTRA!

50

DATE: _____________

ABOUT THE AUTHOR

READ ALL ABOUT IT!

SPECIAL REPORT
EXTRA!
EXTRA!
50
(NAME OF PAPER)
DATE: __________
(HEADING)
(WEATHER HEADLINE)
(DRAWING OF EVENT)
(EVENT DETAILS)
ABOUT THE AUTHOR
(ABOUT ME)
READ ALL ABOUT IT!

SPECIAL REPORT

50

EXTRA! EXTRA!

DATE: ________________

ABOUT THE AUTHOR

READ ALL ABOUT IT!

SPECIAL REPORT

50

EXTRA! EXTRA!

(NAME OF PAPER)

DATE: ________

(HEADLINE)

(WEATHER HEADLINE)

(DRAWING OF EVENT)

(EVENT DETAILS)

ABOUT THE AUTHOR

(ABOUT ME)

READ ALL ABOUT IT!

SPECIAL REPORT

50

EXTRA! EXTRA!

DATE: _______________

ABOUT THE AUTHOR

READ ALL ABOUT IT!

SPECIAL REPORT

(NAME OF PAPER)

DATE: _______________

(HEADLINE)

(WEATHER FORECAST)

(DRAWING OF EVENT)

(EVENT DETAILS)

ABOUT THE AUTHOR

(ABOUT ME)

READ ALL ABOUT IT!

SPECIAL REPORT
EXTRA!
EXTRA!
50
DATE: _______________
ABOUT THE AUTHOR
READ ALL ABOUT IT!

SPECIAL REPORT

EXTRA! EXTRA!

50

(NAME OF PAPER)

DATE: ______________

(HEADLINE)

(WEATHER HEADLINE)

(DRAWING OF EVENT)

(EVENT DETAILS)

ABOUT THE AUTHOR

(ABOUT ME)

READ ALL ABOUT IT!

SPECIAL REPORT

50

EXTRA! EXTRA!

DATE: ______________

ABOUT THE AUTHOR

READ ALL ABOUT IT!

SPECIAL REPORT

50

EXTRA! EXTRA!

(NAME OF PAPER)

DATE: _______________

(HEADLINE)

(WEATHER HEADLINE)

(DRAWING OF EVENT)

(EVENT DETAILS)

ABOUT THE AUTHOR

(ABOUT ME)

READ ALL ABOUT IT!

SPECIAL REPORT

50

EXTRA! EXTRA!

DATE: ___________

ABOUT THE AUTHOR

READ ALL ABOUT IT!

50
SPECIAL REPORT
EXTRA!
EXTRA!
(NAME OF PAPER)
DATE:
(HEADLINE)
(FURTHER HEADLINE)
(DRAWING OF EVENT)
(EVENT DETAILS)
ABOUT THE AUTHOR
(ABOUT ME)
READ ALL ABOUT IT!

SPECIAL REPORT

50

EXTRA! EXTRA!

DATE: _____________

ABOUT THE AUTHOR

READ ALL ABOUT IT!

SPECIAL REPORT

EXTRA! EXTRA!

(NAME OF PAPER)

DATE: ______________

(HEADLINE)

(WEATHER HEADLINE)

(DRAWING OF EVENT)

(EVENT DETAILS)

ABOUT THE AUTHOR

(ABOUT ME)

READ ALL ABOUT IT!

SPECIAL REPORT

50

EXTRA! EXTRA!

DATE: _____________

ABOUT THE AUTHOR

READ ALL ABOUT IT!

SPECIAL REPORT

50

EXTRA! EXTRA!

(NAME OF PAPER)

DATE: ______________

(HEADLINE)

(DRAWING OF EVENT)

(EVENT DETAILS)

(WEATHER HEADLINE)

ABOUT THE AUTHOR

(ABOUT ME)

READ ALL ABOUT IT!

SPECIAL REPORT

EXTRA! EXTRA!

50

DATE: _______________

____

____

ABOUT THE AUTHOR

READ ALL ABOUT IT!

SPECIAL REPORT

50

EXTRA! EXTRA!

(NAME OF PAPER)

DATE: ___________

(HEADLINE)

(WEATHER HEADLINE)

(DRAWING OF EVENT)

(EVENT DETAILS)

ABOUT THE AUTHOR

(ABOUT ME)

READ ALL ABOUT IT!

SPECIAL REPORT

50

EXTRA!
EXTRA!

DATE: _______________

ABOUT THE AUTHOR

READ ALL ABOUT IT!

50

SPECIAL REPORT

EXTRA! EXTRA!

DATE: _______________

(NAME OF PAPER)

(HEADLINE) ___________________________

(WEATHER FORECAST) ___________________________

(DRAWING OF EVENT)

(EVENT DETAILS)
____
____
____
____
____
____
____
____
____
____
____

ABOUT THE AUTHOR

(ABOUT ME)
____
____

READ ALL ABOUT IT!

SPECIAL REPORT

50

EXTRA! EXTRA!

DATE: __________

SPECIAL REPORT

50

EXTRA! EXTRA!

(NAME OF PAPER)

DATE: ___________

(HEADLINE)

(WEATHER HEADLINE)

(DRAWING OF EVENT)

(EVENT DETAILS)

ABOUT THE AUTHOR

(ABOUT ME)

READ ALL ABOUT IT!

SPECIAL REPORT

50

EXTRA! EXTRA!

DATE: ______________

ABOUT THE AUTHOR

READ ALL ABOUT IT!

SPECIAL REPORT

DATE: _______________

ABOUT THE AUTHOR

READ ALL ABOUT IT!

SPECIAL REPORT

50

EXTRA! EXTRA!

DATE: ___________

ABOUT THE AUTHOR

READ ALL ABOUT IT!

SPECIAL REPORT

50

EXTRA!
EXTRA!

(NAME OF PAPER)

DATE: _______________

(HEADLINE)

(WEATHER HEADLINE)

(DRAWING OF EVENT)

(EVENT DETAILS)

ABOUT THE AUTHOR

(ABOUT ME)

READ ALL ABOUT IT!

SPECIAL REPORT

50

EXTRA! EXTRA!

DATE: _______________

ABOUT THE AUTHOR

READ ALL ABOUT IT!

SPECIAL REPORT

EXTRA! EXTRA!

50

(NAME OF PAPER)

DATE: _______________

(HEADLINE)

(WEATHER HEADLINE)

(DRAWING OF EVENT)

(EVENT DETAILS)

ABOUT THE AUTHOR

(ABOUT ME)

READ ALL ABOUT IT!

SPECIAL REPORT

EXTRA! EXTRA!

DATE: ________

ABOUT THE AUTHOR

50

READ ALL ABOUT IT!

SPECIAL REPORT

50

EXTRA! EXTRA!

(NAME OF PAPER)

DATE: _______________

(HEADLINE)

(WEATHER HEADLINE)

(DRAWING OF EVENTS)

(EVENT DETAILS)

ABOUT THE AUTHOR

(ABOUT ME)

READ ALL ABOUT IT!

SPECIAL REPORT

50

**EXTRA!
EXTRA!**

DATE: _______________

🌡️ _______________

ABOUT THE AUTHOR

READ ALL ABOUT IT!

SPECIAL REPORT

EXTRA! EXTRA!

50

(NAME OF PAPER)

DATE: ______________

(HEADLINE)

(WEATHER REPORT)

(DRAWING OR EVENT)

(EVENT DETAILS)

ABOUT THE AUTHOR

(ABOUT ME)

READ ALL ABOUT IT!

SPECIAL REPORT

EXTRA!
EXTRA!

DATE: _______________

ABOUT THE AUTHOR

READ ALL ABOUT IT!

SPECIAL REPORT

50

EXTRA! EXTRA!

(NAME OF PAPER)

DATE: ___________

(HEADLINE)

(WEATHER HEADLINE)

(DRAWING OF EVENT)

(EVENT DETAILS)

ABOUT THE AUTHOR

(ABOUT ME)

READ ALL ABOUT IT!

50

EXTRA!
EXTRA!

DATE: ___________

ABOUT THE AUTHOR

READ ALL ABOUT IT!

SPECIAL REPORT

EXTRA!
EXTRA!

(NAME OF PAPER)

DATE: ________________

(HEADLINE)

(WEATHER REPORT)

(DRAWING OF EVENT)

(EVENT DETAILS)

ABOUT THE AUTHOR

(ABOUT ME)

READ ALL ABOUT IT!

SPECIAL REPORT

50

EXTRA! EXTRA!

DATE: ________________

ABOUT THE AUTHOR

READ ALL ABOUT IT!

SPECIAL REPORT

50

EXTRA! EXTRA!

(NAME OF PAPER)

DATE: _____________

(HEADLINE)

(WEATHER HEADLINE)

(DRAWING OF EVENT)

(EVENT DETAILS)

ABOUT THE AUTHOR

(ABOUT ME)

READ ALL ABOUT IT!

SPECIAL REPORT

50

EXTRA! EXTRA!

DATE: _____________

ABOUT THE AUTHOR

READ ALL ABOUT IT!

SPECIAL REPORT

EXTRA! EXTRA!

50

(NAME OF PAPER)

DATE: ______________

(HEADLINE)

(WEATHER HEADLINE)

(DRAWING OF EVENT)

(EVENT DETAILS)

ABOUT THE AUTHOR

(ABOUT ME)

READ ALL ABOUT IT!

SPECIAL REPORT

50

EXTRA! EXTRA!

DATE: ________

ABOUT THE AUTHOR

READ ALL ABOUT IT!

SPECIAL REPORT

50

EXTRA! EXTRA!

(NAME OF PAPER)

DATE: _______________

(HEADLINE)

(WEATHER HEADLINE)

(DRAWING OF EVENT)

(EVENT DETAILS)

ABOUT THE AUTHOR

(ABOUT ME)

READ ALL ABOUT IT!

SPECIAL REPORT

50

EXTRA! EXTRA!

DATE: _____________

ABOUT THE AUTHOR

READ ALL ABOUT IT!

SPECIAL REPORT

50

EXTRA! EXTRA!

(NAME OF PAPER)

DATE: ___________

(HEADLINE)

(WEATHER REPORT)

(DRAWING OF EVENT)

(EVENT DETAILS)

ABOUT THE AUTHOR

(ABOUT ME)

READ ALL ABOUT IT!

SPECIAL REPORT

50

EXTRA!
EXTRA!

DATE: ____________

ABOUT THE AUTHOR

READ ALL ABOUT IT!

SPECIAL REPORT

50

EXTRA! EXTRA!

(NAME OF PAPER)

DATE: ______________

(HEADLINE)

(WEATHER HEADLINE)

(DRAWING OF EVENT)

(EVENT DETAILS)

ABOUT THE AUTHOR

(ABOUT ME)

READ ALL ABOUT IT!

SPECIAL REPORT

50

EXTRA! EXTRA!

DATE: _______________

ABOUT THE AUTHOR

READ ALL ABOUT IT!

50
SPECIAL REPORT
EXTRA!
EXTRA!
(NAME OF PAPER)
DATE:
(HEADLINE)
(WEATHER HEADLINE)
(DRAWING OF EVENT)
(EVENT DETAILS)
ABOUT THE AUTHOR
(ABOUT ME)
READ ALL ABOUT IT!

SPECIAL REPORT

50

EXTRA! EXTRA!

DATE: ___________

ABOUT THE AUTHOR

READ ALL ABOUT IT!

SPECIAL REPORT

EXTRA!
EXTRA!

(NAME OF PAPER)

DATE: __________

(HEADLINE)

(WEATHER REPORT)

(DRAWING OF EVENT)

(EVENT DETAILS)

ABOUT THE AUTHOR

(ABOUT ME)

READ ALL ABOUT IT!

SPECIAL REPORT

50

EXTRA! EXTRA!

DATE: ________________

ABOUT THE AUTHOR

READ ALL ABOUT IT!

SPECIAL REPORT

50

EXTRA! EXTRA!

(NAME OF PAPER)

DATE: _______________

(HEADLINE)

(WEATHER HEADLINE)

(DRAWING OF EVENT)

(EVENT DETAILS)

ABOUT THE AUTHOR

(ABOUT ME)

READ ALL ABOUT IT!

SPECIAL REPORT

50

EXTRA! EXTRA!

DATE: _______________

ABOUT THE AUTHOR

READ ALL ABOUT IT!

50

SPECIAL REPORT

EXTRA!
EXTRA!

(NAME OF PAPER)

DATE: _____________

(HEADLINE)

(WEATHER HEADLINE)

(DRAWING OF EVENT)

(EVENT DETAILS)

ABOUT THE AUTHOR

(ABOUT ME)

READ ALL ABOUT IT!

SPECIAL REPORT

DATE: ___________

ABOUT THE AUTHOR

READ ALL ABOUT IT!

SPECIAL REPORT

EXTRA!
EXTRA!

50

(NAME OF PAPER)

DATE: ________________

(HEADLINE)

(WEATHER FORECAST)

(DRAWING OF EVENT)

(EVENT DETAILS)

ABOUT THE AUTHOR

(ABOUT ME)

READ ALL ABOUT IT!

SPECIAL REPORT

50

EXTRA! EXTRA!

DATE: ______________

ABOUT THE AUTHOR

READ ALL ABOUT IT!

SPECIAL REPORT

50

EXTRA! EXTRA!

(NAME OF PAPER)

DATE: ________________

(HEADLINE)

(WEATHER HEADLINE)

(DRAWING OF EVENT)

(EVENT DETAILS)

ABOUT THE AUTHOR

(ABOUT ME)

READ ALL ABOUT IT!

SPECIAL REPORT

DATE: _______________

ABOUT THE AUTHOR

READ ALL ABOUT IT!

50
SPECIAL REPORT
EXTRA!
EXTRA!
(NAME OF PAPER)
DATE:
(HEADLINE)
(WEATHER HEADLINE)
(DRAWING OF EVENT)
(EVENT DETAILS)
ABOUT THE AUTHOR
(ABOUT ME)
READ ALL ABOUT IT!

SPECIAL REPORT

50

EXTRA! EXTRA!

DATE: ___________

READ ALL ABOUT IT!

SPECIAL REPORT

50

EXTRA! EXTRA!

(NAME OF PAPER)

DATE: ______________

(HEADLINE)

(WEATHER HEADLINE)

(DRAWING OF EVENT)

(EVENT DETAILS)

ABOUT THE AUTHOR

(ABOUT ME)

READ ALL ABOUT IT!

SPECIAL REPORT

50

EXTRA! EXTRA!

DATE: _______________

ABOUT THE AUTHOR

READ ALL ABOUT IT!

50

SPECIAL REPORT

EXTRA!
EXTRA!

(NAME OF PAPER)

DATE: _______________

(HEADLINE)

(WEATHER HEADLINE)

(DRAWING OF EVENT)

(EVENT DETAILS)

ABOUT THE AUTHOR

(ABOUT ME)

READ ALL ABOUT IT!

SPECIAL REPORT

50

EXTRA!
EXTRA!

DATE: _______________

ABOUT THE AUTHOR

READ ALL ABOUT IT!

SPECIAL REPORT

50
SPECIAL REPORT
EXTRA!
EXTRA!
DATE:
ABOUT THE AUTHOR
READ ALL ABOUT IT!

SPECIAL REPORT

50

EXTRA! EXTRA!

(NAME OF PAPER)

DATE: _____________

(HEADLINE)
____

(WEATHER HEADING)
____

(DRAWING OF EVENT)

(EVENT DETAILS)

ABOUT THE AUTHOR

(ABOUT ME)

READ ALL ABOUT IT!

SPECIAL REPORT

50

EXTRA! EXTRA!

DATE: _______________

ABOUT THE AUTHOR

READ ALL ABOUT IT!

SPECIAL REPORT

EXTRA! EXTRA!

50

(NAME OF PAPER)

DATE: ______________

(HEADLINE)

(WEATHER HEADLINE)

(DRAWING OF EVENT)

(EVENT DETAILS)

ABOUT THE AUTHOR

(ABOUT ME)

READ ALL ABOUT IT!

SPECIAL REPORT

50

EXTRA! EXTRA!

DATE: _____________

ABOUT THE AUTHOR

READ ALL ABOUT IT!

50
SPECIAL REPORT
EXTRA! EXTRA!
(NAME OF PAPER)
DATE: ______
(HEADLINE)
(WEATHER HEADLINE)
(DRAWING OF EVENT)
(EVENT DETAILS)
ABOUT THE AUTHOR
(ABOUT ME)
READ ALL ABOUT IT!